Waiting for the Moon

Poetic Reflections on Nature

Taylor Wray

INSPIREBYTES
OMNI MEDIA

Waiting for the Moon

Distributed globally with Expanded Distribution by KDP.
Cover artwork by Frances Vail.

ISBN Paperback: 978-1-953445-91-9
ISBN E-Book: 978-1-953445-92-6
Library of Congress Control Number: 2020943847

 INSPIREBYTES OMNI MEDIA

Inspirebytes Omni Media LLC
PO Box 988
Wilmette, IL 60091

For more information, please visit Inspirebytes.com.

To my family, for their love and support—always. And to Beth and Christina, for planting the seeds of this book with me all those years and martinis ago.

In life, there are moments that take our breath away and stop us in our tracks—moments that give us pause. They are often awe-filled in the simplest and most unexpected ways. These moments invite us to slow down, look around, and redirect. When we come out of the pause—if we are lucky—we are forever changed.

This was my experience with Taylor Wray's poetry. In only 17 syllables he managed to capture my attention and take up residence in my heart and mind. I could feel myself getting lost in his gift with each word as it revealed itself to me. I immediately knew I wanted to share my experience with others.

In *Waiting for the Moon*, Taylor takes us on a lingering journey through the seasons, and the boat on which we sail is fueled by his imagination, three lines at a time. From frost-covered leaves and dappled sunlight to long, steamy afternoons at the end of summer, Taylor perfectly captures a single relatable moment in time, repeatedly.

Whether you are new to haiku or have spent decades enjoying its complex simplicity, this book of poetic reflections on nature will easily accompany you throughout the year. Each page ushers you in to a new moment, season by season.

It is my hope that you find Taylor's poetry as captivating as I have and that the following pages fill you with both nostalgia and wonder.

Martina E. Faulkner
August 2020

Haiku can be described, in the most basic terms, as a Japanese style of poetry consisting of 17 syllables, split into three lines of five, seven, and five syllables, respectively. At times, the definition is left at that.

The nuances of haiku are more complex, however, and there are additional rules and guidelines that haiku follow to varying degrees. Traditionally, haiku are about nature and contain a seasonal word or reference. (Haiku-style poems that are not about nature are generally categorized as senryū.) Haiku often juxtapose two distinct images or parts— sometimes separated in English-language haiku by punctuation, such as a dash or ellipsis. And frequently, modern haiku do not adhere to any specific syllable count, while still reflecting the spirit of traditional Japanese haiku.

Having said all this, my observation from reading and writing haiku is that there is a range of opinions about what constitutes "real" haiku. It is my belief that there is plenty of room at the table for individual styles and creative expression.

What the different approaches to haiku do have in common is that they capture a specific moment—an observation, a scene, a feeling, a sunlight hits a single leaf in a certain way. Maybe it's the sudden awe experienced when gazing at a crystal-clear night sky. Or it could be the sense of change in the air as summer begins to give way to fall. The ability to convey the immediacy and impact of these moments using a minimum of words gets at what I see as the essence of haiku—and is something that I strive for in my own poetry.

In this collection, I use a conventional seventeen-syllable framework for each poem. Some would argue against such rigidity, but as a writer, I enjoy exploring syntax and sound within a fixed syllable count and appreciate the continuity that it provides from poem to poem. Regardless of the technical details, I hope these short pieces transport the reader into the moments described and felt, and do so in a way that captures the essence of my experiences of—and the power of our collective connection to—the natural world. And mostly: I hope that these small assemblages of syllables inspire readers to explore and embrace the poetry that nature creates for us in every tiny moment.

TMW
July 2020

FALL

Summers, faded now—
Playing barefoot at last light,
Waiting for the moon

Possibility
In the scent of pine and stone
As morning begins

A cracked blue bucket,
Faded under rain-soaked leaves,
One of summer's ghosts

The wind, sharp with smoke,
Soon to dance in golds and reds,
Rich with fall's promise

Watching Orion
Watching me—a brief, bright glimpse
Of the amazing

The rain, in torrents,
Shoos us in reproachfully
For a book and tea

Rainy-day cadence
A minor-key sonata
Befitting the mood

Standing in the dark
In the company of trees
And all that they've seen

Night rain softly speaks,
Its timeless benediction
Balm for the weary

A joyous heartbreak
In the perfect song of this
Electric blue sky

In the predawn dark,
Stars so bright I skip a breath—
Diamonds just for me

The temerity
Of a leaf in golden flight—
Arcing, tumbling, free

Stars weave fantasies
Flecked with fleeting night-magic,
Fading with the dawn

Autumn's graceful bow—
A quiet resolve in this,
The act of dying

WINTER

Winter waltzes in
All frosted rust and flocked gold
As fall fades to white

Crescent moon, atilt,
Balanced just so, bright vessel
Of collected dreams

Ombré sky at dawn—
Quiet, watercolor grace
Smooths our sharp edges

Steam dances, rising,
A cup's offering of warmth
Greeting falling snow

A lone, rogue snowflake
Pirouettes in on the wind—
One last sunlit dance

Past winter's dark fields—
A rush of cold and woodsmoke,
The stars resplendent

Crystalline night sky,
An Arctic gift of silver—
Orion stands tall

Splatter-paint moonbeams
Seep through shadows in cryptic,
Luminous mazes

Cool, snow-blanketed
Shadows cast jealous glances
At sun-mottled grass

The sun at zenith
Fells winter's crystal armor
In drip-drop cascades

Slivers of moonlight
Through the old pines, snow-bent boughs
Silently dreaming

Snow-dampened quiet
Reveals nighttime tree whispers
And hushed, dark footfalls

Under perfect stars,
Doubt succumbs to awe as night
Unfurls her splendor

Snow-melt rivulets
Sketch shimmering galaxies
On a glass canvas

Pale leaf, autumn's ghost,
Frozen in winter's embrace,
Longs for spring's release

SPRING

Beneath the full moon
A ragged V spills northward
Chasing spring whispers

A quick-change artist,
March breeds delight and despair
In equal measure

Rain sings vernal songs
Of wet stone and waking earth
Carried on the wind

Spring staggers forward
Sodden, mud-slicked, shivering—
Approaching slowly

Verdant abundance,
Still waking, merely stirring,
Awaits spring's clean sweep

Leaves tremble, waiting,
A huddled mass soon scattered
By spring's primal roar

Dewy petals blush,
Spreading in florid display,
Craving spring's caress

April's deception—
A showman's deft spring flourish,
Frost tucked in his sleeve

Twitchy-tailed tumblers
Playing silent-film charades,
Springtime's merry fools

Lemon-zest yellows,
Vibrant greens, spilling across
Spring's fragrant canvas

April's dying gasp
As May roars to victory,
Riding waves of green

Dandelion wisps
Tumble and surge, a maelstrom
Of wide-eyed wishes

Bursts of blooms dazzle,
Floral fireworks aglow
In pop-sizzle hues

A certain magic
Amid blushing smears of sky
Approaching gloaming

Whispers of lilacs,
Heavy with the weight of night—
The moon in hiding

SUMMER

This hammock's-eye view,
A fresco of blues and greens—
The wind's soft brushstrokes

Night drive, an old song,
Past farms, fragrant in the dark—
Summer unfolding

Underneath the oak
Midday shade is savored, sweet,
Like summer's first plum

Petrichor windsong,
Rich notes of clay and flora,
Heralding the storm

Lotus, fiercely pink,
Emerges from dark waters,
An awakening

The trail bends ahead,
Out of sight, shying away
From the sun's queries

A trick of moonlight—
Silhouettes cascade, spilled ink
Dancing on the lake

Wet sidewalks, steamy
With summer heat—quiet now
As the city breathes

The smell of ripe peach—
Each juicy bite brimming with
Sweet revelation

Straying from the now,
Lost in honeysuckle dreams
Of summer's nightsong

Opulent blossoms,
Spring's lavish ephemera,
Dim with the dog days

Summer hangs heavy
In these woods—seeping, verdant,
Filling each hot breath

August's corn stands high,
Row upon green row, unbowed
At summer's fading

Beneath dark ripples
Shimmering dreams coalesce
In the quiet deep

On a cool morning
In August, imagining
The glory of fall

Truly, I have so much to be grateful for and so many people to thank. (And hopefully I have done so outside the pages of this volume.) But in particular, I'd like to thank Martina Faulkner, my publisher, for inviting me to join her on IOM's journey and for believing in my poetry enough to envision this book's existence. Her enthusiasm and wisdom have helped me through many moments of self-doubt during the publication process. Quite literally, my book wouldn't have happened without her.

I would also like to thank the Twitter writing community. When I very tentatively began sharing my poetry online, these generous writers were quick to welcome me and lend their support and suggestions. I've learned so much from writing in such amazingly talented company and continue to be inspired by their work every day. Thank you.

As a Nashville-born transplant to Rochester, New York, Taylor Wray has found short-form poetry to be the perfect antidote to the long, cold winters. Writing his own brand of haiku and senryū, he creates snapshots of his observations, thoughts, and feelings, 17 syllables at a time.

Follow Taylor Wray online at:

twitter.com/inthreelines
instagram.com/inthreelines
facebook.com/inthreelines

Made in the USA
Monee, IL
22 September 2020

43202002R00083